CHEROKEE

P9-DFA-193

Take a Deep Breath

What Is CO$_2$?

Library of Congress Cataloging-in-Publication Data

Morrison, Yvonne.
  Take a deep breath : what is CO_2? / by Yvonne Morrison.
    p. cm. -- (Shockwave)
  Includes index.
  ISBN-10: 0-531-17790-4 (lib. bdg.)
  ISBN-13: 978-0-531-17790-7 (lib. bdg.)
  ISBN-10: 0-531-15483-1 (pbk.)
  ISBN-13: 978-0-531-15483-0 (pbk.)

  1. Carbon dioxide--Juvenile literature. 2. Atmospheric carbon dioxide--
Juvenile literature. 3. Carbon dioxide--Environmental aspects--Juvenile literature.
I. Title. II. Series.

  QD181.C1M67 2007
  551.51'12--dc22

2007012404

Published in 2008 by Children's Press, an imprint of Scholastic Inc.,
557 Broadway, New York, New York 10012
www.scholastic.com

SCHOLASTIC, CHILDREN'S PRESS, and associated logos are trademarks
and/or registered trademarks of Scholastic Inc.

08 09 10 11 12 13 14 15 16 17
10 9 8 7 6 5 4 3 2 1

Printed in China through Colorcraft Ltd., Hong Kong

Author: Yvonne Morrison
Educational Consultant: Ian Morrison
Editor: Mary Atkinson
Designer: Matthew Alexander
Photo Researcher: Mary Atkinson

Photographs by: Big Stock Photo (p. 5; forest, p. 11; seashell, peeling orange, p. 19; cows,
p. 23); **Getty Images** (smoggy city, cover background; p. 12; geyser, p. 15; firefighters,
pp. 18–19; p. 21; flood, p. 23; pp. 24–26; cyclists, traffic, pp. 28–29); **Jennifer and Brian
Lupton** (teenagers, pp. 32–33); **Photolibrary** (p. 3; p. 8; marine diatoms, p. 11; pp. 13–14;
car exhaust, p. 15; p. 16; soda water, p. 17; p. 27; two girls, p. 29; pp. 30–31; ship, pp. 32–33);
Tranz: Corbis (p. 7; girl, p. 17); Reuters (woman, cover)

All illustrations and other photographs © Weldon Owen Education Inc.

SHOCKWAVE
SCIENCE

Take a Deep Breath

What Is CO_2?

Yvonne Morrison

children's press®

An imprint of Scholastic Inc.

NEW YORK • TORONTO • LONDON • AUCKLAND • SYDNEY
MEXICO CITY • NEW DELHI • HONG KONG
DANBURY, CONNECTICUT

CHECK THESE OUT!

SHOCKER
Stuff to Shock,
Surprise, and
Amaze You

Quick Recaps
and Notable
Notes

Word Stunners
and Other Oddities

The Heads-Up
on Expert Reading

Links to More
Information

CONTENTS

atmosphere (*AT muhss feer*) a mixture of gases surrounding a planet

fossil fuel a fuel, such as coal, oil, or natural gas, that formed over a long time from the remains of plants and animals

greenhouse gas any gas in the atmosphere that absorbs heat and warms up the earth. Greenhouse gases occur both naturally and as a result of human activity.

photosynthesis (*foh toh SIN thuh siss*) the process by which green plants use energy from sunlight to convert carbon dioxide and water into food and oxygen

respiration (*ress puh RAY shuhn*) the process of breaking down food to release energy. It involves breathing, or taking in oxygen and releasing carbon dioxide.

· ·

For additional vocabulary, see Glossary on page 34.

The word *atmosphere* comes from the Greek *atmos*, meaning "vapor," and *spharia*, meaning "sphere." *Atmosphere* was first used in connection with the moon. But, we now know that the moon has no atmosphere!

The gasoline we put into cars is a **fossil fuel**.

About four hundred years ago, Belgian chemist Jan Baptist van Helmont discovered an invisible substance. He called it "wild spirit." He had been burning charcoal in an airtight jar. When he finished, he found that the weight of the ash was less than the weight of the charcoal that had burned. From this, he figured out that some of the charcoal must have been turned into an invisible substance.

Van Helmont's wild spirit is what we now call carbon-dioxide gas. Carbon dioxide is a **compound**. It is made up of one carbon **atom** joined to two oxygen atoms. It is often known simply by its **chemical** formula: CO_2.

At the temperatures and pressures found on the earth, CO_2 is always a gas. It makes up a small part of our **atmosphere**. CO_2 gas is invisible. It has no smell, and it won't burn. It is also one of the most important gases on the planet. Without CO_2, life would not be possible.

Scientists sometimes represent a CO_2 molecule as three round atoms linked in a line. Here, the carbon atom in the middle is white, and the two oxygen atoms are red.

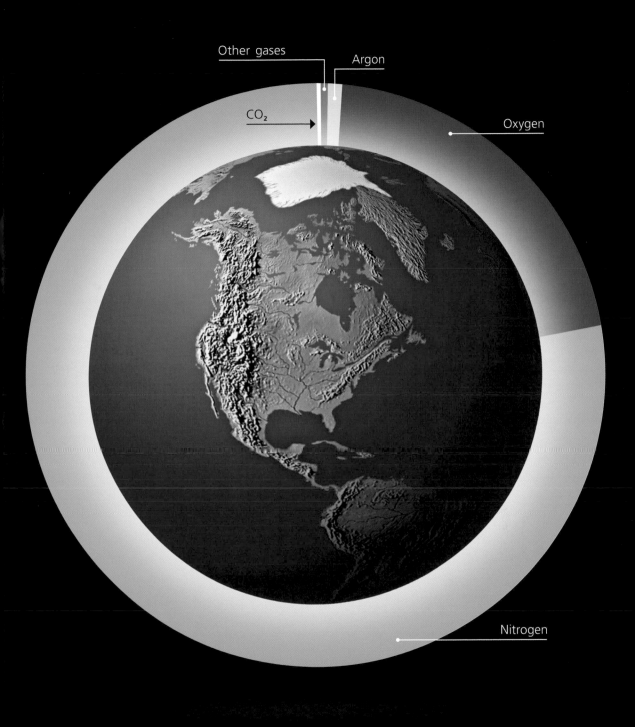

This diagram shows the relative amounts of the different gases in the earth's atmosphere. For example, the light blue represents nitrogen, and the thin white line represents CO_2. CO_2 makes up only about 0.03 percent – that's about one CO_2 atom for every 3,333 atoms in the air.

9

No CO$_2$, No Life on Earth!

All green plants take in CO$_2$. They use energy from sunlight to convert CO$_2$ and water into oxygen and sugar. The oxygen is released into the atmosphere, and the sugar becomes food for the plant. This process is called **photosynthesis**.

Plants could not grow without the sugar they get from photosynthesis. Animals, including humans, are also dependent on photosynthesis. This is because plants are at the bottom of most food chains. To survive, animals must eat plants or be part of a food chain that began with a plant.

Plants make their own food, and animals eat food. Plants and animals may get food in different ways, but they *use* food in the same way. All living things need to break down their food in order to get energy from it. Plants and animals both do this through a process called **cellular respiration**. This process uses up oxygen and produces CO$_2$.

CO$_2$ is released into the atmosphere by plants and animals as part of a process called **respiration**, or breathing. (Many people do not realize that plants breathe too!) Both plants and animals take in air to get the oxygen they need. Then they release CO$_2$ into the atmosphere. Plants do not give off very much CO$_2$, however. They take in much more through photosynthesis than they give off through respiration.

Photosynthesis: CO$_2$ + water + energy $\longrightarrow$ sugar + oxygen

Cellular respiration: sugar + oxygen $\longrightarrow$ CO$_2$ + water + energy

Look at these two chemical equations. They show that the reactions of photosynthesis and cellular respiration are the reverse of one another.

Growing plants give off much more oxygen than they take in. One tree produces approximately enough oxygen to support two people. This is one of the reasons why forests are so important.

It is not just land plants that make food using photosynthesis. **Phytoplankton**, shown here magnified 25 times, use photosynthesis as well. They **absorb** CO_2 dissolved in the ocean. Algae and some **bacteria** use photosynthesis too.

As Dry as Ice

At very low temperatures (below −109 °F), CO_2 turns from a gas into a solid called dry ice. It is an extremely cold, hard substance. It is called dry ice because it looks like ice (frozen water), but it does not melt into a liquid the way ice does. Instead, it changes directly into a gas. This process is called **sublimation**.

CO_2 is found in its liquid state only at very high pressures. These pressures are not usually found naturally on earth. As soon as the pressure is released, the CO_2 turns back to either a gas or dry ice, depending on the temperature.

Some Ways We Use Dry Ice

- cooling food products during transportation
- producing fog for special effects
- cleaning surfaces (by blasting them with tiny pellets of dry ice)
- encouraging rainfall by seeding clouds
- cooling high-power computer systems
- preventing explosions in the fuel tanks of jet aircraft

The fog used for special effects in theatrical productions and rock concerts is created by dry ice. When moist air touches dry ice, the water vapor in the air turns into visible drops of liquid water. The result is dense fog.

I've seen shows where magicians have all this smoke-like stuff on stage. Now I know what it is. It's great to be able to make these sorts of connections.

When dry ice is put into a liquid, such as water, it immediately begins to turn back into gas. This creates violent bubbles in the liquid. Special-effects experts use dry ice to make bubbling potions.

SHOCKER

Dry ice can be dangerous. In an enclosed room, dry ice turns back into a gas, which can fill the room and suffocate any people inside. Dry ice is so cold that it can give you frostbite if you touch it. If you're using it, always wear gloves and have good ventilation!

Where Does CO₂ Come From?

The earth: Most of the CO_2 in the earth's atmosphere came out of volcanoes billions of years ago. Even today, volcanoes are releasing CO_2. **Geothermal** sites, such as the geysers, hot springs, and mud pools in Yellowstone National Park, also release CO_2 into the atmosphere. In some places where CO_2 bubbles up through mineral springs, it makes the water naturally fizzy. This kind of water is sometimes sold as sparkling mineral water – and it is often very expensive!

Burning: Most of the human-produced CO_2 comes from the burning of wood and **fossil fuels**, such as gasoline, oil, and coal. People burn these fuels to produce energy for electricity production, heating, and transportation.

Living things: Most living things produce CO_2 during respiration. When living things die, bacteria and fungi break them down. During this process, they convert the carbon in a dead plant or animal into CO_2, which is released into the atmosphere.

Chemical reactions: Many **chemical reactions**, such as one that takes place in the production of cement, produce CO_2. Mixing an acid with a carbonate (a substance containing carbon and oxygen) produces a lot of bubbly CO_2. You can do this yourself by mixing vinegar (an acid) with baking soda (a carbonate). But take care – the results can be quite dramatic! Some factories use this process to clean up waste. Instead of pumping harmful acids into wastewater, they mix the acids with a carbonate, such as chalk or limestone, producing CO_2 and water.

Chalk is a carbonate. When it is placed in hydrochloric acid, it dissolves, giving off bubbles of CO_2.

Exhaust is mainly nitrogen, CO_2, and water vapor. It also contains pollutants, such as hydrocarbons, which consist of unburned and partly burned fuel particles.

A buildup of underground steam mixed with CO_2 causes Old Faithful geyser in Yellowstone Park, Wyoming, to erupt at regular intervals. A plume of boiling water as high as 184 feet bursts from the ground about every 80 minutes.

Did You Know?

A person breathes out about 100 gallons of CO_2 every day. This CO_2 weighs about 2 pounds.

What Can You Do With CO_2?

The first person to create a **carbonated** drink was a chemist named Joseph Priestly. Although people already knew about naturally sparkling water, no one had ever tried making a fizzy drink using chemical reactions. Then, in 1772, Priestly mixed sulfuric acid and limestone (a carbonate). He bubbled the resulting CO_2 through water. Sure enough, he had a fizzy drink!

These days, carbonated drinks are very popular. In fact, more than a quarter of all the drinks Americans consume are sodas. On average, we each consume more than 60 gallons of it each year! Store-bought drinks are carbonated by mixing CO_2 gas with flavored water. The mixture is then sealed under pressure. When you open the drink, you release the pressure. Some of the dissolved CO_2 escapes, producing the familiar fizzing sound, as well as bubbles. Unfortunately, drinking too many sodas is bad for your health. Sodas are acidic and can cause tooth decay. They also contain additives and large amounts of sugar. Drinking large amounts of soda is not a healthy choice.

Joseph Priestly

How We Get the Fizz

1. CO_2 is mixed with water.
2. The mixture is sealed under pressure.
3. We open the drink and release the pressure.
4. We hear the escaping CO_2 fizz.

Next time you open a bottle of soda, take a look at what happens. Before you open the bottle, you probably won't see many bubbles. However, as soon as the pressure is released, the CO_2 will start bubbling up.

Burp!

You've just guzzled down a can of soda. Suddenly, you feel a lot of pressure in your belly. You open your mouth, and ... BURRRRP!

Your burp is made up mostly of all the CO_2 that you swallowed in the soda. The excess CO_2 in your stomach is forced up through your throat and out your mouth. If you try to keep yourself from burping, you might get a sour taste and a stinging feeling in your mouth. That is because the CO_2 has reacted with your saliva to form a weak acid. It is better for your health to let it out!

17

Because CO_2 is heavier than
air and doesn't burn, it is often used
in fire extinguishers. The dense CO_2 blankets the fire, depriving it
of the oxygen it needs in order to burn. As a result, the fire goes out.

CO_2 has uses in many industries. It is used in the production of aspirin
and in metalworking. In aerosol cans, it is used as a **propellant**. CO_2 is what
makes canned whipped cream come out light and fluffy. It is also used
to blow up self-inflating life rafts.

Baking soda and yeast produce bubbles of CO_2 that make breads and cakes
rise. CO_2 is also used to take the caffeine out of coffee. Many indigestion
remedies produce bubbles of CO_2 when the dry ingredients (an acid and
a carbonate) are mixed with water.

One new use for liquid CO_2 is in the dry-cleaning process. Many dry cleaners
use poisonous chlorine products to dissolve grease stains. Some, however,
are starting to use less-harmful liquid CO_2 to clean clothes. Unfortunately,
it takes a lot of pressure to make CO_2 remain in liquid form, so laundries
need to install special washing machines to convert to CO_2 dry cleaning.

Uses of CO₂:
- sodas
- fire extinguishers
- dry cleaning
- in aerosol cans
- self-inflating rafts
- making bread rise

Shellfish use calcium combined with CO₂ from the ocean to make their hard shell homes!

Plastic From Oranges

Scientists in the United States have discovered a way to make plastics from orange-peel oil and CO₂. To date, almost all plastics have been made from gasoline products. But gasoline is a nonrenewable resource. Oranges, on the other hand, are renewable. The scientists believe that we should collect CO₂ waste from factories instead of releasing it into the atmosphere. This CO₂ could then be used to make plastics from renewable resources such as orange-peel oil.

CO$_2$ Pollution

Clean, fresh air is about 0.03 percent CO$_2$. CO$_2$ is harmless at this level, but it becomes dangerous at higher concentrations. CO$_2$ pollution is a problem in some buildings where people work in closed offices. Breathing air with high concentrations of CO$_2$ (about 0.2 percent or more) can make people feel drowsy, nauseous, and headachy. Still higher concentrations (about 7 percent) can lead to unconsciousness and death. In the past, coal miners faced constant danger because there are often pockets of air with high concentrations of CO$_2$ in mines. Today, many miners have detectors that monitor the air in mines.

The amount of CO$_2$ in the atmosphere has changed over time. Cold water absorbs more CO$_2$ than warm water. This means that during the ice ages, the oceans were able to absorb more CO$_2$, and so there was less CO$_2$ in the atmosphere. Over the last 150 years, humans have increased the amount of CO$_2$ in the atmosphere by more than 30 percent. This elevated CO$_2$ level is due to several factors. Among these are the increased burning of fossil fuels; certain manufacturing processes, such as the production of concrete; and the widespread burning of forests to make way for farms. The increase is not enough to make people sick, but it could have a drastic effect on the climate.

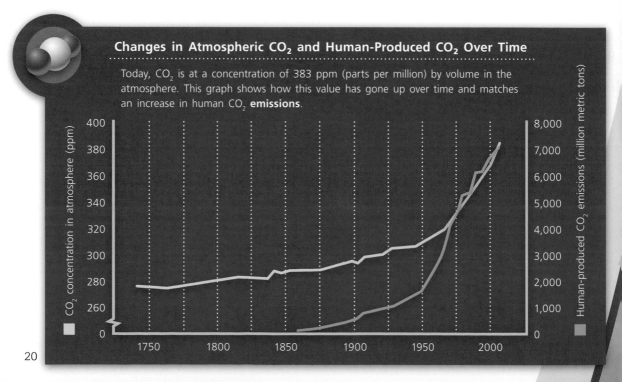

Changes in Atmospheric CO$_2$ and Human-Produced CO$_2$ Over Time

Today, CO$_2$ is at a concentration of 383 ppm (parts per million) by volume in the atmosphere. This graph shows how this value has gone up over time and matches an increase in human CO$_2$ **emissions**.

How do scientists measure the amount of CO_2 that was in the atmosphere hundreds or thousands of years ago? The answer is found in cold places, such as Antarctica. Scientists drill out long tubes of ice. These ice cores contain trapped bubbles of air from long ago.

It can be difficult to remember when to use the words *amount* and *number*. Generally, if it can be counted, we use *number*. For example, we say *number of CO_2 molecules* but *amount of CO_2*.

Many people in Beijing, China, often walk to work through thick **smog**. Some countries, such as China, have a rapidly increasing amount of industry and a greater number of cars on their roads. Many developing countries need the industry and find it hard to afford the cost of reducing the amount of pollution they produce.

21

Warming Up

Many scientists around the world are worried that an increase in CO_2 will cause major changes to our **climate**. They are concerned that it will lead to **global warming**.

The earth and its atmosphere are constantly absorbing energy from the sun's rays and emitting some of this energy in the form of heat. Some gases in the atmosphere, such as nitrogen and oxygen, don't absorb heat well. Others, called **greenhouse gases**, absorb a significant amount of heat. These gases include CO_2, water vapor, **CFCs**, and methane. These greenhouse gases keep the planet warm. It is a good thing we have them in our atmosphere; otherwise, the planet would be too cold to support life.

The problem is that the earth's temperatures are on average 1 °F warmer than they were 100 years ago. Many scientists think this is caused by an increase in the amount of greenhouse gases in the atmosphere, and that this is caused by human activities. Warmer weather might sound quite pleasant, especially in wintertime. But if the earth warms by just a few degrees, the glaciers and polar ice caps will melt. This could cause the sea level to rise, flooding coastlines. Warming the atmosphere might also lead to an increase in weather-related problems, such as storms. Warm oceans are a breeding ground for hurricanes and other wild weather.

The Greenhouse Effect

1. The sun's rays reach the earth through the atmosphere, providing energy for all living things.

2. Some of the sun's heat energy is **absorbed** by the earth, which then radiates heat back into the atmosphere.

3. Some of that heat energy is absorbed by greenhouse gases. It helps to keep the earth warm. The rest of the energy goes into outer space.

The 11,500 people living on the Pacific islands of Tuvalu are experiencing many floods, extra-high tides, and cyclones. Many islanders blame these occurrences on an increase in greenhouse gases. If the conditions continue to worsen, residents will need to leave the islands and find new homes.

SHOCKER

All of the volcanoes in the world belching out CO_2 release only one-hundredth the amount of CO_2 that humans produce!

When cows digest grass or hay, they burp a lot, which releases the greenhouse gas methane into the atmosphere. It has been estimated that the average cow releases about 600 quarts of methane a day!

The Great Climate Debate

Global warming is a very hard thing to prove. Why? First of all, climate is a hard thing to understand. The weather changes every day – long-term climate change takes a long time to track. An enormous number of factors, many of which are not yet fully understood, affect the climate and the atmosphere. Changing one thing, such as the amount of CO_2 in the atmosphere, could affect other things in unexpected ways.

Not all scientists agree about global warming. Some do not think that global warming has much to do with human activity. They say that the temperature is rising naturally, as it has been doing since the last ice age.

The author is asking a question after the first sentence. I don't think she expects me to answer it. I think she is using it to gain my interest. It works for me!

No Fishing

In Harbor

Lake Mead in Nevada provides water for the city of Las Vegas, the state of Arizona, and southern California. The coincidence of a dramatic population increase and a drought has resulted in the lake's lowest water levels since the 1960s. Some say that the drought is caused by global warming. Others say that it is a natural event.

A few scientists think that the earth will cool itself. They think that the warmer air will cause more water to **evaporate** from the oceans. This water will then form thick clouds, which will block some of the sunlight. There are even scientists who think that global warming is good, since more plants will grow to feed the earth's people.

Recent studies, however, have provided more evidence to support the idea that the human production of greenhouse gases is leading to global warming – and that global warming will cause problems for us. Most of the world's scientists now believe this. And many of the world's people agree that we shouldn't wait until we know for sure. If CO_2 production really is a problem, they want to reduce it before it's too late.

In some places, such as England (below), increasingly severe floods are being blamed by some scientists on global warming. They say that the bad weather is caused by a change in high-level airflow caused by an increase in greenhouse gases. Others say there is not yet enough evidence to prove this.

Cutting Back on Fossil Fuels

The Kyoto treaty is an international agreement aimed at reducing greenhouse-gas production. It has been signed by 169 countries. However, because of the high costs involved, many countries – even some of those that signed the agreement – have failed to cut back on their emissions.

It is difficult and expensive to reduce CO_2 production, because humans rely on fossil fuels in so many ways. We use fossil fuels to heat our homes, power our cars, and produce electricity. Research into other ways of doing these things is expensive. But already there are alternatives. Electricity can be produced using wind, solar, or wave power instead of by burning coal. There are hybrid cars on our streets, which run on electricity as well as gas. A hybrid car uses very little gas because its engine is combined with an electric generator that charges a battery as the car drives. Engineers have also developed cars that run on hydrogen gas. These cars may become available in the future.

Many of the cars on our roads contain only one person. Carpooling and better use of public transportation would reduce traffic jams and pollution.

Individual people can make a difference. Using public transportation consumes less fuel than using cars. For short trips, walking can be a good choice. You can save electricity by turning off lights, computers, and TVs that you're not using, and by opening windows rather than using air conditioning. Recycling and reusing products helps save on the energy needed to produce new products.

Walking to school is good for keeping in shape as well as looking after the environment. Just make sure you keep safe at all times. Walking with friends is a good idea.

These cyclists in the Philippines took part in a bike-a-thon to raise support for their government's campaign to reduce greenhouse-gas emissions.

Soaking Up CO_2

Many people around the world are working hard to think of new ways to reduce the amount of CO_2 in the atmosphere. Many forests, which are important consumers of CO_2, are being cut down. In order to counteract this, some businesses are now selling "carbon credits." A customer uses a spreadsheet to work out how much CO_2 he or she produces each year. This amount depends on how much fossil fuel the person uses for heating, transportation, and electricity. The customer then pays the company to plant enough trees to remove the same amount of CO_2 from the atmosphere. Some people think that this is not enough to make a difference. Others think that if many people do it, it will soon have an effect.

There are other ways to reduce the CO_2 in the air. Some engineers have investigated the idea of trapping CO_2 underground. When natural gas or oil is pumped up from underground, huge empty pockets are left behind. It might be possible to fill these pockets with extra CO_2 instead of releasing it into the atmosphere. However, this solution could be very expensive.

Oceans and growing plants soak up CO_2, but they can't take in enough. Some scientists have suggested adding nutrients to the ocean to feed phytoplankton. These tiny water plants might then flourish and take in large amounts of extra CO_2. However, studies would need to be done to figure out what other problems this might lead to.

Plenty of other ideas for preventing global warming have been suggested. A few scientists would like to see giant mirrors orbiting the earth to reflect extra sunlight away. Others have suggested doing the same job with billions of small lenses.

On average, a person living in the U.S., Canada, or Australia produces about ten times as much CO_2 in a year as a person living in Asia.

This illustration shows what a giant mirror in space might look like. To change the earth's climate, and reduce global warming, many mirrors would be needed. How well this would work and what other problems might result from it are unknown.

These schoolchildren in California took part in a global-warming community rally in Los Angeles. They helped plant trees and other plants in a park. The plants will help reduce the amount of CO_2 in the atmosphere.

CO$_2$ in the Solar System

Earth is certainly not the only planet in the solar system with CO$_2$. In fact, the atmosphere of Venus contains 96 percent CO$_2$! This massive amount of CO$_2$ has caused a runaway greenhouse effect, making the surface of Venus a blistering 870°F. Venus is hotter even than Mercury, which is the closest planet to the sun.

Venus is sometimes called Earth's sister planet, because it is nearly the same size as Earth. How did it come to have such a different atmosphere? On Earth, the oceans remove a lot of CO$_2$ from the atmosphere. This can't happen on Venus because it has no oceans. Because the planet is so much closer to the sun than Earth, all the water on it evaporated a long time ago. Venus also has many volcanoes, which are constantly releasing CO$_2$.

Earth's other neighbor, Mars, also has a high percentage of CO$_2$ in its atmosphere – about 95 percent. But the atmosphere of Mars is very thin. There is not enough gas in the atmosphere to absorb a significant amount of heat. The temperatures on Mars are, on average, much colder than those on Earth. Often it is so cold that the carbon dioxide in the air turns to dry ice and falls as "snow."

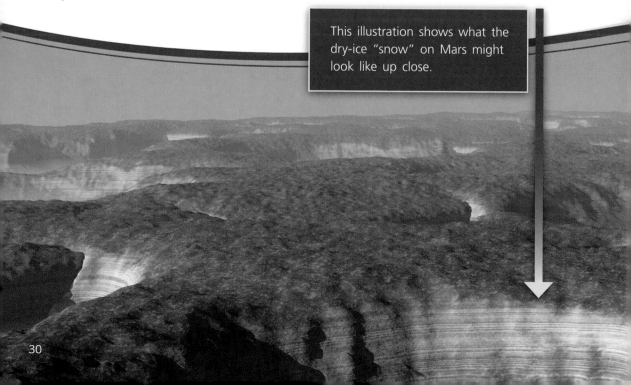

This illustration shows what the dry-ice "snow" on Mars might look like up close.

Many scientists think that the atmosphere of Mars is a lot like the atmosphere Earth had when it was first formed billions of years ago. Some scientists think that this means that we could **terraform** Mars, turning it into another Earth, which could support plant and animal life. To do this, ways would need to be found to produce more greenhouse gases to thicken and warm the atmosphere. Then plants could grow, converting some of the CO_2 into oxygen and food. It would take hundreds of years to create an atmosphere on Mars like that on Earth, but it is thought to be possible. Some people think we should try it. Others think that Mars should be left alone. Changing its atmosphere would most likely kill off any undiscovered bacteria or other life forms that might already live there.

Venus is similar in size to Earth, but its atmosphere is very different. The high level of CO_2 heats the planet hotter than an oven. Thick clouds of sulphuric acid add to the greenhouse effect.

In words like *terraform*, *terra-* means "land" or "earth." Related words include: *terrain*, *terrarium*, and *extraterrestrial*.

Did You Know?

CO_2 is found on the moons of the outer planets too. These moons are so cold that all the CO_2 is solid dry ice.

When scientists change the earth to suit humans, it is called geo-engineering. Geo-engineering used to be thought of as a crazy idea. Most scientists laughed at the thought of using giant sunshades to shield the earth from sunlight. They thought that firing tiny particles into the air to reflect sunlight into space (right) was ridiculous. But now many people are so worried about global warming that they are starting to consider these alternatives.

WHAT DO YOU THINK?

Should governments spend money on geo-engineering?

PRO

If global warming is going to be a problem in the future, we need to come up with a plan now. If we wait, it will be too late. We may never need to use geo-engineering, but if we do, it's better to be prepared.

This is an artist's impression of a warship firing reflective particles into the atmosphere.

Should we be spending money on complicated schemes to try to cool the earth? What if they don't work? What if a solution ends up causing more problems for the environment than it fixes? This is a possibility. For example, one scientist suggested pumping sulfur gas into the atmosphere to cool the planet, but another scientist pointed out that this might harm the ozone layer!

CON

Geo-engineering is expensive and no one knows if we're going to need it or if it will work. It's a waste of money and could cause more problems than it fixes. The money could be better spent on finding ways to reduce the amount of greenhouse gases that we produce.

GLOSSARY

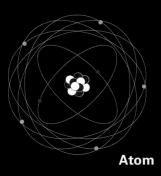

Atom

absorb to take in

atom the smallest amount of an element that still has the properties of that element

bacteria single-celled organisms that cannot be seen without a microscope

carbonated combined with CO_2

cellular respiration the part of the overall process of respiration that takes place inside cells; the breakdown of food and oxygen to produce water, energy, and CO_2

CFCs chlorofluorocarbons; chemicals containing chlorine, fluorine, carbon, and sometimes hydrogen, which damage the ozone layer in the atmosphere

chemical (*KEM uh kuhl*) related to, or produced by, chemistry, which is the study of substances

chemical reaction a process that changes one or more substances into one or more different substances

climate the usual weather in a place

compound a substance made up of atoms of two or more elements linked together

emission (*ee MISH uhn*) a substance released into the atmosphere

evaporate to change from a liquid into a gas or vapor

geothermal (*gee o THER muhl*) to do with the heat inside the earth

global warming a gradual rise in the temperature of the earth's atmosphere

phytoplankton (*FI toh plank tin*) microscopic ocean plants

propellant a compressed gas or liquid used to disperse the contents of an aerosol can

smog a mixture of smoke and fog that hangs in the air over large cities and industrial areas

sublimation the process of changing from a solid to a gas without going through a liquid stage

terraform to change a planet so that it is able to support an atmosphere and climate similar to that of Earth

FIND OUT MORE

BOOKS

Conley, Kate A. *Joseph Priestly and the Discovery of Oxygen*. Mitchell Lane Publishers, 2005.

Harman, Rebecca. *Carbon-Oxygen and Nitrogen Cycles*. Heinemann Library, 2005.

Minkel, Dan. *Global Warming*. Greenhaven Press, 2006.

Morrison, Yvonne. *Earth Matters*. Scholastic Inc., 2008.

Simon, Seymour and Smithsonian Institution. *Lungs: Your Respiratory System*. HarperCollins, 2007.

Tocci, Salvatore. *Carbon*. Children's Press, 2005.

WEB SITES

Go to the Web sites below to learn more about global warming.

www.epa.gov/climatechange/kids

www.pewclimate.org/global-warming-basics/kidspage.cfm

www.dnr.state.wi.us/org/caer/ce/eek/earth/air/global.htm

www.icbe.com/carbonforkids

http://tiki.oneworld.net/pollution/pollution_home.html

INDEX

ABOUT THE AUTHOR

Yvonne Morrison is fascinated by science. In fact, she was a scientist before becoming a writer. One Halloween, she brought some dry ice home from the lab to make special effects at a party. The guests were amazed! Yvonne lives with her husband in an old-fashioned cottage in a sunny seaside town in New Zealand. Her hobbies are dancing, listening to music, collecting antiques, and reading.